Talking To Myself

Cariann Briley

BookLeaf Publishing

India | USA | UK

Presentation by *BookLeaf Publishing*

Web: www.bookleafpub.com

E-mail: info@bookleafpub.com

ISBN: 9789360945152

First edition 2024

DEDICATION

I dedicate these poems to my husband for encouraging me to cry, feel, express, and share all of my feelings. Thank you for accepting all of me.

PREFACE

This book is filled with poems about feeling each and every one of our emotions and expressing them all. No more stuffing down our feelings, no more ignoring the tingle up our spines, these poems are about allowing all of our emotions to flow through each of us.

Table of Contents

Overachiever

Pale and shaking
I walk
My hand on the wall
One foot in front of the other

An insistent voice
Yelling, in my head
Wait!
Don't take a nap! Don't rest!

Let's go for a walk
Let's get some sun
Let's get it done! We can do it!
Says my overachiever

I actually stop
And listen
but not today,
Ha! I choke out

She drops her head
Then jumps into a tirade
You are lazy! You can't get anything done!
You'll never finish anything!

Little O, I say
You can go 'DO' whatever you like
I can, she asks
Yes, you can

As long
As it does not require
Our brain, our body
Or our soul

O K
Really, anything?
But what will I do without our brain, our body,
Or our soul?

You could go work on our book
I could?
Uh-huh
Without our mind, body or soul?

Yep, I say
She jumps for joy
I can I can I can
Wait a minute…

How will you know what I do?
You won't know!
Yes, I will
How?

You'll tell me
Right after I rest
Yes, Yes, Yes
I will tell you!

OK OK OK
I am off!
She runs away
Lightning sparks fly

I reach my bed
I lay down my head
And I
Rest

Expectations

I once read
having expectations
breeds disappointment.

If we never
have expectations,
we can never
be disappointed.

As if
being disappointed
serves no purpose.

What if
being disappointed
gives new direction?

Yes
feeling disappointed
can send us to our knees
halt us on our path

Then
open your eyes to see
lift your ears to listen

feel with your heart

A
new direction
new action
new expectation.

Rage

I can feel it inside of me
it is growing

Sulking and prodding
Lurking and goading

Always
trying to escape
fighting
every ounce of my control

It sneaks out
in snaps bites and growls

Sometimes
it gains control

Sometimes I want to let it loose
let them fear its wrath
Give it all my strength
And turn away

But if it overtook me
I would scream and fight

and scream and fight
and scream some more

I am not sure I could stop
so much rage built up
I would scream until I cried
I might scream until I died

Will it ever
go away

Wash away
Slither away

And leave me
whole or broken
I don't care
just

Leave
Me

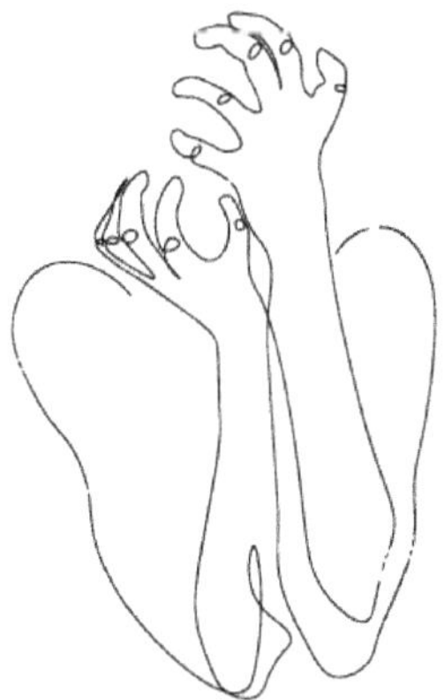

Restless

The itchy crawling
Under my skin
Feeling

The can't be still
Wiggling my toes
Feeling

The give me space
Don't touch me
Feeling

The all out of sorts
Wrong in my skin
Feeling

The I need to
Dash out the door
Simmer in the Sun
Melt with the Moon
Slide through the Stars
Feeling

Restless no more

I Exist

I exist
I EXIST
I exist

Whether you want me to or not
Whether you acknowledge me or not
Whether you listen to me or not

I exist
I EXIST
I exist

Whether you see me or not
Whether you hear me or not
Whether you hurt me or not

I exist
I EXIST
I exist

Whether you like me or not
Whether you fight me or not
Whether you lie to me or not

I exist

I EXIST
I exist

Whether you dream of me or not
Whether you fear me or not
Whether you dare me or not

I exist
I EXIST
I exist

Release

It's bubbling up inside me
Boiling bubbles rising
Higher and higher
Hotter and hotter

It's burning up inside me
Searing liquid rising
Sharper and sharper
Farther and farther

It's lava dragging me under
Molten liquid coiling
Around and around
Bound and bound

It's swallowing me under
Rock hardening tightening
Harder and Harder
Tighter and Tighter

I'm cracking breaking myself out
Moving cracking straining
Fighting and Fighting
Screaming and Screaming

Breaking and Breaking
Breathing and Breathing
Bubbles release rising
I'm freeing myself

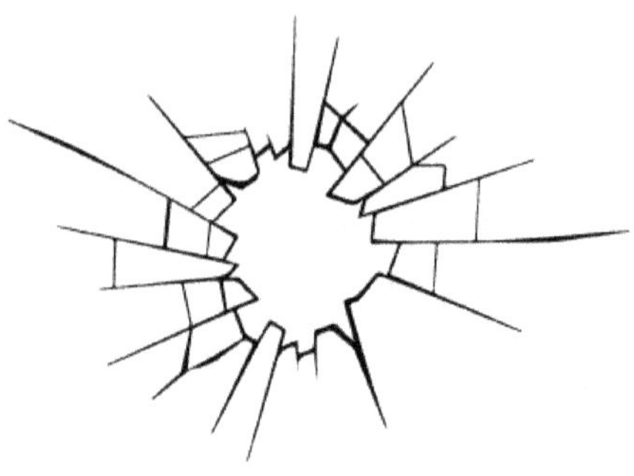

Stirring

A collision
Arms caught her
Bodies lingered
As he held her

A look
Into stirring green eyes
Her skin tingled where
He had touched her

An energy stirred
Humming along her arms
Colors vibrated around her
He filled her vision

A stranger
Stirring her desire
Awakening her from slumber
His soul whispered to hers

A knowing
Stirred along her spine
Crept into her heart
He would be a part of her

Forever and always

The Eye of the Storm

Those niggling wriggling insistent thoughts
Swirling whirling hair raising thoughts
Ricocheting around ALL my other thoughts

My heart rate climbing
My thighs perspiring!
My nerves racing

Go away!
Why do you stay?!
Just go away, I say!

Around and around and around it goes
A whirling dervish tornado it grows
Grimacing its monster teeth it shows

My mind is reeling
My soul is crying
My skin is crawling

Go away!
Why do you stay?!
Just go away, I scream!

Stranded in the storm for these moments

Can't breath, can't see for these moments
Fall to the ground, hide from it all
In these moments

Feels like forever
And the end is never
The sun is gone forever

As the sobs subside
And the tears dry
The skies open up and cry

The wind settles
The sound quiets
My resistance softens

The moment passes
My feeling detaches
My thought dances

I can hold it
See it
Touch it

Express it

Terror

Words whispered on the wind
A caress along my cheek
My hair flips up on end
Goosebumps run down my skin

A memory shudders
I'm frozen, sliding away
Shivering, ice in my veins

Darkness descends, numbing
Don't move don't speak don't tell
Tears silently spill
Blinding light, blinding pain

The world is spinning
Rushing by in a blur
The hands of terror push
Hold me down, trapped

Everyone is walking by
No will to fight
Only my mind can flee
Away to my safe place

Far away and alone

Days go by, weeks go by
Somehow someway
The ice melts

For a moment
Terror
Lifts his heavy hands
Away

Sadness

19

Sadness
lies buried beneath
the layers of my rage
dig deep into
my darkness

My little girl is crying
alone in the dark
Sadness

Return

Return to the abandoned child
Recover the broken pieces
Reclaim the stolen (violated) self
Rebuild post-destruction
Rediscover within the darkness
Release in a flood of tears

Pain

It doesn't take much
To send me back to that child
Paper and pen
A moment hidden
Comes from the past

Flying backwards
Through time
Numbing tingling dizzying

My head is throbbing
My eyes are heavy
Let's go lie down
Forget we exist

The pain will go away
The pain doesn't have a face

I try to resist
Sludge through the mud
My voice squeaking
Nothing makes it better
It's all just pain—more pain

Staring into the Dark

Staring into the dark
Blankets heavy
Kick kick kick
Need to move

It's late
Everyone
But me
Is sleeping

The house is heavy
With their dreams
The tiny noises
Press in on me

Why doesn't sleep
Come for me
Why doesn't sleep
Take me

Staring into the dark
The seconds
Tick tick tick
I try not to move

It's getting late
Everyone
But me
Is dreaming

The house is heavy
With ghosts walking
The floors creaking
They lean in on me

Why doesn't sleep
Wait for me
Why doesn't sleep
Come for me

Staring into the dark
My lips dry
Lick lick lick
Swallow my throat thick

It's early now
Everyone
But me
Is stirring

The house is gray
As night turns to day
The sun rising
Streams through

Sleep has taken me
Sleep has come for me
Its grip tight;
Clinging to me

Staring into the dark

To the Finish

Step off the edge
Slide tumble and roll
Past the fear
Skid your way to the finish

Get up off the ground
Dirty scraped and bleeding
Past the pain
Push your way to the finish

Keep going through the mud
Stumbling lost and confused
Past the doubt
Crawl your way to the finish

Run through the tape
Thirsty, starved, exhausted
Past the dread
Bust your way to the finish

But wait
What did you finish?
Who did you leave behind?
Where are you going?
Now that you have finished.

Alone

Alone
all the people outside
here I sit
alone

Silence
in every room
here I sit
silent

Stuck
the weight heavy
here I sit
stuck

Exhausted
but can't sleep
here I sit
exhausted

Sad
deep darkness descends
here I sit
sad

Desperate
not a single movement
here I sit
desperate

Alone
JUST DO SOMETHING ANYTHING
here I sit
alone

Cliff

Step off the cliff
Step off, she says to me
How long have we been
Standing here?
How many years?

Twenty
I say
Not taking my eyes off the edge

She breaks out of my skin
She is laughing shimmering floating

What's the worst that could happen?!
Death? I doubt you'll even get a bruise!

I stare down at the long jagged edge
She is floating over

Seriously?

I glare at her
Jealous
Envious
Hateful

Of her light

I don't understand
The fear that holds me here
How could she understand
The fear that holds me here

She tries to push me, shove me,
To move my feet for me
She is light as air
I rise on my toes ever so slightly
She huffs and sits leaning against me
Pouting
Murmuring

She hates being stuck up here
As much as I do
The wind is
Swooshing
Swirling

Holding me here
Steadily going nowhere

Citrus

The cool soft skin
Heavy to the touch
Some soft, some tough

Slice through skin
Juice running down the knife
Breathe the citrus tang

The bright orange vibrant
Hold the rough skin
Pressing down

Destroy the orange
Squashing, squeezing
To drink the juice

My mouth waters
Tightens readying for the tang
Thirst rising up

Sheer and utter sunshine
Citrus joy on my tongue
The pure gold liquid tingling

Surrender

As the darkness descends
As the shadow swirls
As the light leaves

Grab a pen
Grab paper
Grab hope

Write it out; write it all
Write on and on and on

Soak up the darkness
Soak up the shadows
Soak up the lights

Let it bleed
Let it pour
Let it flow

On to the paper
On to the witness
On to the world

Surrender to the darkness
Surrender to the shadow
Surrender to the light

The Beginning and the End

Run
Run for your life

Don't
Don't risk your life

Burn
Burn it all down

Start
Start all over

Leave
Leave it all behind

Ask
Ask me to risk my life

When
When you can't not take a drink

It's
It's easier for me to leave

Then

Then for you to not drink

Feels
Feels like the beginning of the end

Always
Always the beginning and the end

That Moment

When the world skids to a halt
When everything you knew is untrue

When you are on the knife's edge
When you begin to see all the lies

When you lose all of yourself
When all the trust—in others in you
Becomes vaporized

When all control is lost
When all your illusions of power
Become stolen

When you hate those you loved
When the violence screams and the rages rises
Becomes uncontrollable

When you are gripped in despair
When the dead weight of the pain
Becomes unbearable

Bare it
Share it
Wear it

Dare it
Tear it

When you are ready
After steady slow steps
When you are ready to take back your power
Take it all back and grow

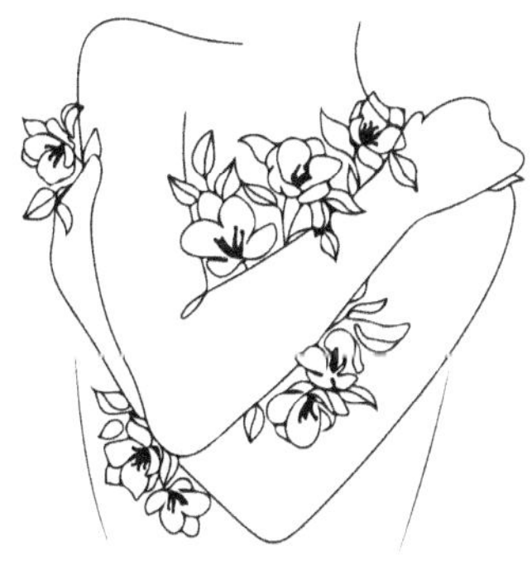

Holding Space

I pour out my darkness
Spilling all over
Drenching him
Drowning myself

And here he stands
Rooted grounded
His arms wrapped around me
Holding me up

I empty every tear
Sob
Image of fear
Until I am nothing

And here he stands
Solid and present
Witnessing my pain
Holding it for me

I settle into a calm
My words surrounding us
His beating and open heart
Holding all of me

www.ingramcontent.com/pod-product-compliance
Lightning Source LLC
LaVergne TN
LVHW010917200726
843509LV00013B/1970